Transforming the Field

D1125715